MW01644657

Things I Hold Onto…

A Collection of Poetry

by

Ariana Iverson

Thing's I Hold Onto

ISBN: 9798339453543

Thing's I Hold Onto

This is dedicated to the Lovers and the Fighters. Because fighting for what you love will ALWAYS be the true testimony.

Thing's I Hold Onto

Thing's I Hold Onto

CONTENTS

	A Message	i
Ch. 1	Trauma	Pg 1
Ch. 2	Unrequited Love	Pg 34
Ch. 3	Sacred Energy Xchange	Pg 70
Ch. 4	Me	Pg 85

Thing's I Hold Onto

Thing's I Hold Onto

A MESSAGE

You have to make mistakes

In order to learn

Remember that life is meant to teach you

So, when you feel down

Read this again

Thing's I Hold Onto

CHAPTER 1
HOLDING ONTO…

TRUAMA

My confessions

I was a self-sabotaging control freak

I didn't realize my power: so, I allowed myself to shrink.
To fit in or go unnoticed.
I played in the background (Literally and Figuratively)

I disregard the fact that my energy speaks louder than my words.

I've battled with
Depression
Anxiety
And a brief eating disorder

I am sensitive.

I cry when I'm angry.

I lacked boundaries.

I scare myself out of opening up and getting too close to others out of fear of losing them and myself.

Every day is a battle. Every day I am learning how to be myself without overthinking it. To allow others in my life without putting a time limit. Learning how to be present in my everyday moments whether I think it's good or bad.

My goal isn't to teach, coach or counsel. I simply want to share my experiences and hopefully someone can find inspiration and power to transform their lives.

I'm still learning how to ask for what I deserve without feeling guilty for it

THINGS I HOLD ONTO

Reflecting on Karma

My tragedies Birthed poetry

Pain, manipulation and fear

Were thrown into the fire

I now stroke that fire with compassion

Compassion for myself to heal

From wounds that I created

I had to learn that I attracted reflections of me

In people

places

and things

They were reflections of secrets I held onto in the back of my mind

Trying to trick myself. Thinking I could hide from them

But just like the moon reflecting off the water

I saw myself deep down in the murky depths of souls

Lost and confused. Wondering! How did we get here?

It had me questioning

Who sent you? Who told you to come through

and wreak havoc on my life on my mind

Then I realized I put the call in

And the universe answered

It heard me from underneath the noise

Not able to truly decipher what I wanted

Because I gave it contradicting thoughts

THINGS I HOLD ONTO

So, it sent reflections

Leaving me to deal with my karma

So hurt and tired I had to disappear. I had to go into the darkness. Jumping into those murky dangerous seas

So, I could save the lost girl drowning Before life decided to let her sink. I pulled her up

I watched her finally breath Choking on air mixed with tears

Happy that life sends lessons in those tragedies

Giving a second chance To live life again

Changes have to be made

People have to be replaced

But it's all in the name of the game

One day we'll realize exactly why

things were never

meant

to be the same

A Conundrum

They Say
Hurt people
hurt People
More like damaged People
Do more Damage to people

Alice no Wonder

I Remember all of those things we
used to say to each other
The things that left butterflies
Fluttering through the pits of my stomach

Something happened that day
I ate the forbidden fruit
And all the butterflies
Died

Choking on words left unsaid
Actions undone
Regurgitating hurt
I'm trying to rewind time
But I'm lost
Wondering like Alice
In a land of curiosity
Fables
Fairy Tales
And mystical stories
Trying to find my way out

Kintsugi

I let broken inside of my body
I allowed it to tell me lies
To keep me broken inside
It told me stories that I knew wasn't true
But somehow I couldn't pick myself up fast enough
So broken made a home inside of my womb
It got cozy
Setting fires to my insecurities
Yelling and screaming in my head
There was something about this verbal abuse

I let broken inside of my body
Thinking somehow I could put the pieces back together again
Filling them with gold perfection
To somehow create a masterpiece
They call that kintsugi
The old Japanese art of taking broken pieces and filling them with gold

To make them whole again
Art is not supposed to be beautiful
Art is supposed to be felt
Art is supposed to be seen
In all of its imperfect perfection

I let broken inside of my body
Neither one of us wanted to be broken
But no one wants to admit that they are broken
Afraid of how the world will judge them
If they aren't anything but a beautiful masterpiece

I am not a victim
I am not a martyr
I'm someone who knows what broken feels like
To hit rock bottom
Just so I can look up and see the light
Broken pieces are a part of the story

So I let broken inside of my body
I let it make love to my mind
It stole my heart
Scattered it throughout the universe
I'm finding pieces of me amongst the stars
Healing myself and sharing it for the world to see
I am broken
But I am complete

Rhetorical Questions

Some days I catch myself wondering
Wondering why I'm not married yet
Like damn not one guy I've been with
thought I was the one
Like damnnnn you don't want to wake up
next to me for the rest of your life

Sharing your dreams
Like I don't feed your soul
I know I can be a little difficult
But damn am I not wife material

Don't answer that
It was rhetorical

But I can't help but to wonder

Some days I catch myself wondering
Wondering why I don't have any kids yet
Like isn't this the age when they just start popping out
Like is my biological clock broke or something
It has me questioning
Like Why am I not ready for them

I wonder if I'll ever be

Some days I catch myself wondering
Wondering why I'm not her yet
Why am I not the super woman version of me?
The one that can handle any situation
The one that saves the day when the day needs saving
Where is she?
Am I not woman enough?

Then I stopped wondering
And just listened
I can't be everything to everybody
But I can be everything
I NEED

Stand Your ground

There are going to be many people who don't believe in you
They are going to request and demand you change your
dreams and goals to fit their perception

But it's up to you to recognize that their perspective
doesn't define your life
And you will be doing a huge discredit to yourself if you
give up
In order to make them feel comfortable
Self-Note 2020

Shattered Reflections

I stared at my reflection
Long and hard
Staring at the beauty marks, the scars
Staring at the pain behind my eyes
I practice smiling in the mirror
To remind myself what a friendly face looks like
I find my thoughts
Walking around these structured walls
Like a maze I'm trying to find my way out
But I keep hitting the wall

Face planting into the poison ivy that covers them
It's seeps into my mind
It's trying to tell me to stop
I hear it
The louder it gets
The more I realize it's not real
It's all in my head

The poison ivy is like people
Who tell you lies they told themselves
Their words linger in your mind
Cutting through the best parts of you

Through the shattered pieces
I see a new me
Someone who embodies
The good
The bad
And the ugly
I realized that the reflection of me
Can be anything I want to see
I'm no longer afraid
To stare at the reflection
Of me

<u>Disconnected Connections</u>

Everybody loves social media
Showcasing the glitz and glam

But what about the true story
The one you can't see
with a camera in your hand

The story where you're alone
You're crying
No one seems to know

That you're actually struggling
Struggling to keep it all together
Struggling to keep from making decisions
That could cause life changing tethering

What if I showed you the real behind the scenes?
Would you still be proud of me?
Or would it remind you too much of the lies
You try to hide
Just for likes, comments and IGTV

What do you do when love forgets to
meet you at the door
It forgets to shower you with gifts
You thought you deserved

Love decided it no longer lives here
It doesn't want to take up space
In unwanted areas
There's no connection here

It's like when Instagram goes down
And all you see is the refresh screen
You press and release
Just to be met with the same screen

Blank spaces
Just like Blank faces
A reminder of what was supposed to be
I'm not perfect

THINGS I HOLD ONTO

Really no one is
But for enough likes, shares and followers
I can give you the updated version of me
The one that no one gets to see

As if scrolling through social media
Provides a real life for you
It's kind of like what Drake said
About people showing you pictures of people
they don't even really know

Reposting pictures of that vacation they took
But they fail to mention
when they get home
They are really broke

Not just with money
But in spirit
Because when they log off that screen
It's back to reality!

Disconnected connections
creating
Disconnected energy

Empty

I was reminded today that
There is no one here to wipe my tears
There is no shoulder to cry on

No hand to hold
No body to hug
When I need the affection

It's just me
In an empty room
Filled with things
That don't belong to me

Confessions

Have you confessed your sins?

Instamoments

I had a moment
I questioned myself
I almost let the negative
thoughts takeover
I saw her
She was beautiful
She's not me
I started to wonder
why I couldn't get your attention
Like she did

I allowed myself
To dissect my insides
I shattered my appearance in an instance
Damn I haven't felt this way in a long time
I've been confident
I know I'm the shit

But in just a click of a button
All the good things I felt about me
Went sour
Leaving a pain in the bottom of my stomach

I wandered

Why this little voice in my head is trying
so hard to make me feel unworthy

How could I let one image of someone else
Destroy how I feel about me
I tried to drown out the negative self-talk
But it crept back in
Like water
Flowing onto the boat
From the hole I accidentally kicked in

THINGS I HOLD ONTO

It's consuming me fast
I don't want to sink
But then I remembered that I could swim
I reminded myself that I don't have to be
Anyone but me
That I can readjust to my environment
That I am a Queen
I am beautiful
Smart
And resourceful
I don't need to be anyone but me

We are all battling demons
Others can't see
So why compare

Sometimes you have to allow yourself to fall
To be reminded of who you really are
But don't beat yourself up in the moments
When you let your human side takeover

It's just a reminder
you are still alive

And you are beautiful
Even if it's just in your own eyes
Because how you feel about you
Will be reflected back
by the company you keep

Reset

It's like hitting the reset button
A sense of renewal
A new you
In just a flip of a switch

Recognize you reap
What you sow
And when the springtime comes
Things will
Grow
But it's the work you put in before
That helps crack the codes

THINGS I HOLD ONTO

Clarity Spirit

Who are you when the lights go off

When it's dark out

And The sun doesn't shine

If you could make a wish on a thousand stars

How long do you think it would take you to get everything you want?

Do you chase your dreams in the daytime

Or are you afraid of your own shadow

I wonder if you know what the calm before the storm really feels like

When the sky turns grey it thunders and shakes the foundation

Leaving cracks, In the seams of reality

Shooting lighting from the ground

Just in case you were about to lose your mind

I picked a pocket full of dandelions

For you to make a wish

I forgot they disperse. From the first brush of wind

Blame it on sober thoughts

With a drunken pen staring through the looking glass of misery

Can you see clearly? Can you see what your worth is

Do you know what real work is

Removing internal pressure, Going with your gut

moving through fear. Releasing the ego

That's how you get your confidence back

I wish you clarity in your spirit

Vulnerability

Vulnerability is being able to share my deepest thoughts
With a world that is already covered in insecurities
I want to tell you how scared I am
How lonely it can be
How sometimes I'm not sure what I'm doing
My fears and my secrets
I want to share them with one person
No stipulations
No conditions

Just up-front
Real talk
Real personal
I want to tell you everything without fear or judgement
Not necessarily looking for advice
but a shoulder to cry on when necessary
I am the strong one in my life
But sometimes I want to remove the barriers
I want to tear down these walls
And just express how I feel
Raw and deep
Vulnerability

WYKYK

Faith isn't just about believing in yourself or someone else

I'm learning that when I say "I believe IN"

It makes the experience an outer body disconnected idea

I'm practicing the art of knowing

When you know it comes from within

There is no outer force that takes control

It's just you

It's to be aware of your own capabilities

To know is unwavering

There is a truth beyond the minimal understanding

When You Know You Know

Insecure(Maybe)

I'm not sure
As I sit in the middle of an empty room
Thoughts running through my mind
I'm trying to make life decisions
Before I run out of time
I'm not sure
Maybe I'm insecure

<u>Good Dick Lies</u>

Attached to a dead spirit
Prepared and ready to manipulate you out your thoughts
Will fuck you so good mentally and physically
You don't even realize that you're being
Controlled by false words
Living in a fantasy

Trauma Stories

I grew up with 2 sets of parents. Both of my parents remarried. Each household had its own form of toxicity, trauma, abuse and lack of love. Yes! there were "Happy, Peaceful" days but let's be clear; some days left the child me afraid of going home. It left me afraid of using my voice out of fear that someone else would lash out about my words.

And in all honesty, I told myself that I was going to be the opposite of those fears as I entered "adulthood", but I found solace in the very arms of men and women that were exactly what I was hiding from

- Dec 31, 2020

CRUEL SUMMER

I think about Summer days
Burning hot like fresh clothes out the dryer
Most days I wish to just put my toes in the sand
Listening to the crashing of waves all around me
The pungent smell of saltwater
Mix in the breeze

But these days are from those
That I reminisce on
No longer am I hearing the waves
They have been drowned out by screams and protest

Sirens
Screeching

It smells like fire and hatred
Love and war
All I see is black and blue
And I can't breath

The summer air is stale here
No taste no flavor

There's no movement here
Bodies are laid out
Lifeless

The summer has a funny way of scorching
Love affairs
That weren't meant to be

Dousing pain with gasoline
The sun burns hot
It ignites on sight

The burning of flesh
Never leaves your memory

Leaving reminder that life is death
And that's bittersweet

They wanted this to be a hot girl summer
But 2020
Showed how cruel the summer could really be

<u>Cycles and B(lessons)</u>

I keep asking myself "what am I doing wrong?" like who did I piss off

I've been struggling for so long

It's just a part of the story

But the more I try to turn the page

The story doesn't change

It's like a tear in the seams Or a song that skips

Replaying the same sound over and over

Driving me crazy

How do I get out of here?

I don't have the answer for myself

So, I look to others for help

They can't save me

They just keep telling me the same thing

I want to wake up from this bad dream

I created a nightmare

But there's no prayer I can say that will wake me up

There are no miracles for someone like me

I'm not even sure what I deserve these days

I don't know how to escape. I know nothing

There is no magic. No portal that opens, ready for me to step into a new dimension

It's just me

Right here, right now. Left to deal with a lesson

Tears of the Day

I spent the day crying

Like ugly tears

Streaming down my face

As I rode down the street

It was something about

The cleanse that I needed

It was like I spent the day

Confessing and washing my sins away

THINGS I HOLD ONTO

Rhetorical Excuses

He told me to please excuse his hands

He's just a man

Like I gave him a dance. Like he just threw some bands

Tell me Mr. man

How would you feel if I was your sister? And I came to tell you another

Mister

Took it upon himself to misuse his power. And overpowered me

And that he forced me down

Put his dirty hand over my mouth to drown out the sound

And once he was finished all he could muster up and say

Was please excuse my hands that he was just a man

And I shouldn't be looking. That way

Or what if I was your mother

And I told you the story about. This real tall dark skin brother

And how one day I was headed to school

But he enticed me with breaking all the rules

So, he took me home with him. And before I could tell him NO

I want to go home he pushed me down. And took my innocence away

And 9 months later. Out you came

And every day that I look in your face

I see the man that took my life away

How would you feel?

If I was your daughter and every time, I lay in my bed at night you hear my cries

THINGS I HOLD ONTO

And you wonder why but I can't tell my father

That another man raped his daughter and it's my fault

Because I'm the woman. And as it stands a man will just be a man

See these are stories women are all too familiar with

She silently suffers

Because she thought she would be protected by her brother. Not by blood but by a strong black man. Someone she thought she trusted

As a woman. I can't be too nice

I can't be too rude

I can't be too sexy

And I can't be a prude

I can't be too covered up

But I can't be nude

I can't be too smart

Or I might intimidate you

So, you tell me as a man. Why Should I really excuse your hands?

When every day I wake up

I have to fight to be seen

I have to fight to be heard

To be respected. To be loved

To be treated as an equal

My question to you is, are you prepared to protect the black Queen

Are you willing to step up and be a King. Because you have a duty to being more

Than just a man who has a problem with his damn hands

You may think that your life is falling apart
But if you change your perspective, you'll see that life is
falling together. Don't let what you perceive to be negative
Take you out of the game!
Self-note 2020

Monsters Under the Bed

I was lost in the wilderness

In a state of bliss

Away from the rest of the world

That somehow manages to pass

Judgement on things they just don't get

Instead of saying they don't understand

They would much rather point fingers

And make you seem like you're the boogie man

Crazy

Weird

Awkward

Whatever you want to call it

So, I went into hiding

Shielding my love from the world

Jaded and green with envy

That they can live their lives

As if nothing was wrong on their side

But who am I to judge or call them out on their flaws?

I'm just a monster under the bed

Only coming out at night

To feast on the hopeless and the brain dead

Buried Roots

We all have our own stories
My trauma was buried deep
And my family are the roots
Trauma made me stronger
Like the branches on the tree
When the leaves decide to leave

I spent some time with my naked shadow
And honestly, she's pretty cool

She drinks
She smokes
She curses up a storm
She might even slap you
She has spiritual mob ties
And those Negus are fools

Creating from the words of life
She showed me I can grow
Taller and Stronger
When I drop
Low hanging fruit

Trees have so much history
They hold the truths
They help us breath and they feed our souls
They are abundantly giving
Like Christmas trees on Christmas Eve

Adam and Eve ate the forbidden fruit
It gave us vision to see life
Like 2020
It gave us a clear eye view

For the Kid in You

I'm armed with star dust in my veins
Shooting verses out of my throat
I am Shel Silverstein moving the mind through poetic imagery
A little off but on the spectrum
I write through my anxiety
I am the Dr Suess
for the child in you!
The ones that grew up with the 90's complex
Those ones that were told that the future was ours
Then we were pushed Off the porch
I hope in your moments of uncertainty
You are reminded that you can create

CHAPTER 2
HOLDING ONTO...

Unrequited Love

Love & Affection

My love language is peace
Bring me peace
I want to feel safe in your essence
Your presence
To know that I don't have to compete with another for your love and affection

Confessions of a Serial Lover

I have a confession to make
As I take a look back
on the men and women
I've dated
I recognize there's a pattern
I have a thing for artist
It's something about someone baring their soul
on a canvas, in a song or through their words

Someone who uses their creativity
To battle their demons
Yet they do it so eloquently
For the whole world to see
We would use each other as our personal muses
They will paint my words
Illustrating the deepest love ever known
To know that there are people
In this world that have art in their home
That was inspired by the likes of me
We share our love
Giving pieces of each other so freely
I love the artist
Or is it the art?
At this point I'm not even sure

Because once we finish posing
And the strokes of the pen
Have nothing left to give
We're left wondering
If this love is actually meant to be
Is there enough color in the world
To paint the pain, we caused each other
After we use each other up

THINGS I HOLD ONTO

For a display of false love
But it looks good once we've finished

I hope to one day marry an artist
And every day we find new ways
To etch love into our skin
To display the good, bad and ugly
Of our encounters
We will love and respect
The art for what it is
They will paint my soul

As I express their heART
Through words only I know

We are the yin and yang of creative expression
Finding balance through the things
That brought us together

Empty Bottles of Promises

Floating in the ocean
There's no message to be found inside
No lies left to be told or sold
For half price on the black market
There is no auction here for love lost
Just empty promises
Locked away
In a glass bottle
Left to float across the sea
Waiting for someone to pick it up
And fill it with everything they need

I loved you like I would lose you tomorrow
You loved me as if I was going to be here forever
Self-note 2019

<u>Russian Roulette</u>

Mister mister
May the odds ever be in your favor
Playing Russian roulette with
Your life comes at a price
I'd be sad if I had to be the one
To make you meet your maker

I never meant to hurt you
I just wanted to know what you looked like inside

Staring god herself in the eyes
You realize
That yo' lies can't
Hide the truth inside

When you take off your mask
What does your face really look like?

Are you everything I thought you could be
Or are you just a figment of my Imagination?

I have a bad habit of creating things
only I can see

I had imaginary friends growing up
And I think you might be
one of them
My thoughts personified
Only I can see you for who you really are
Broken and vulnerable
Just like me

Living a life full of dreams
Chasing after ghost
With the hopes that they could be
Lovers and friends

THINGS I HOLD ONTO

Soulmates entangled
Spider Webs of lies
Silk
Kisses

I don't want to miss you
I don't want to miss this

But just like the black widow
I couldn't help but devour you

The story begins and ends

BANG
BANG
I shot you down
I only wanted to fix yo' crown
I only wanted to make yo' momma proud

The weight of the world
Keeps trying to tear us apart
Ripping hearts out of chest

What a beautiful mess

Mister
MISTER
I never meant to hurt you
I just wanted to know
What you looked like inside

Soulmate

No one wants to be reminded of a love lost
We want to find love that lasts
A once in a lifetime kind of feeling
Someone who knows you
And loves you for you

A smart man knows that with the right woman by his side
Everything they touch will multiply
She is the missing rib from his side
Waiting to be put back into her place
Treated as an equal
Treated as if she was missed and needed
She knows life is a team effort
A soulmate
Twin flame

Track Meets

A serial lover is who I have been
I wore the identity
Almost like a badge of honor
I had convinced my self
That I was a hopeless romantic
And that's why I was in that space
Being so desperate for love
I missed all the signs that said
To abort this mission
Love is missing
It's only lust
Thoughts created in my head
Of what I imagined could be the real thing
But I realized that I have to compete for your love
I have to take part in the race
I'm doing the 20-yard dash to the finish line
But life is a marathon not a race
And honestly, I don't even like to run
I don't want to engage in the chase
I don't want to try to make things work
If they can't flow easily
It means it's not meant to be
I don't want to force it
But a part of me can't help it
You flash a smile
Touch me just right
And I forget about everything else
I enter the cycle again
Right back to the line
Waiting for the marksman to say
"On your marks, get set, GO!"

Mr. Fix It

You fix everything about the problem

Except the problem

Trying to find new ways to change the circumstances instead

Of looking at it for what it is

Toxic Fairy

i know
you know
that i know
you're no
good for me
does that sound confusing?

i love you
and i know you love me too
but what is love
when we know
we're really no good for each other

we are in a constant
toxic cycle
our starting point is always great
but
as the earth does its pirouettes around the sun
and exposes our weaknesses
i realize how sick of you i am
like the revolver spinning
playing russian roulette with our lives
it's the mind games
the manipulation
that drives me insane

you're like a toxic fairy
sprinkling dust
on everything you touch
how childish of me to still believe in fairies
but what's even worse is still believing that we can change
we won't change
because we're not meant for each other
we are toxic
all the warnings have been signed
sealed and delivered
yet we open the package everyday
praying that something new would come true

Perceptions

I had to learn to stop loving

people by the way that I see them

My perception of you is not real

RollerCoasters

Keep yo' hands inside the ride at all times
I don't want to be confused
By who's hands touched who

Relationships are like rollercoaster rides
When you first get on
You're nervous
Not sure what this ride will do

But as it takes off
You find yourself a little more relaxed in bliss
It starts off slow
Taking you up
The views are nice from here

But just like the crescendo
The drop comes
And your falling
Twisting
And turning
Being pulled in so many directions

You're laughing
Screaming
And for some even crying

Moment by moment
You're questioning yourself
"When is it going to end?"

Toys

Never say never
But I say never put anything
Past a person
Whose been damaged
To the point of no return

They have no regards for life
They don't know how to move beyond
Their pain
No communication
Just puppets pretending to be happy
And little kids pulling the strings

Sorry

The only thing I'm sorry for
Is giving you way more of me
Then I was able to receive

Intimidation Aside

I should have known you wasn't shit
All the times you said that you were intimidated
Just another excuse for you not to be a man
And man up

You would rather fuck with
"Women" who haven't figured out
How to respond without giggling first
You told me you were
Intimidated by a grown ass woman
Someone that can take pipe, cook dinner
build business
pretty much your wife

But you don't have a problem opening
your mouth to ask if you can get your dick sucked

Intimidation aside

You know exactly what to say to take me on a ride
Wild goose chasing with you
But every once in a while
I get a glimpse of life without you
And I'm left wondering

Why the fuck haven't I left yet?
What kind of voodoo hood shit does
This broke no ambition
having ass nigga have on me

It can't be the dick

Can it?!

I'm stronger than that
So, I think
Maybe it's me
I think that I can fix you

THINGS I HOLD ONTO

You're like a science project
But more like an
Experimentation gone wrong

You're like that one-time I tried super glue some shit
and accidentally glued my fingers together instead

Trying to take the easy way around
Has me ignoring all the warnings

Like the "Do Not Enter" sign was made for the blind

You were telling me out of your own mouth
that you weren't ready
But I took that as code word for teach me

So, I tried to put the bullshit aside
And every time I realize the weaker
I get the more I just let shit slide

"He loves me, and I love him"
It sounds good

But my insides rip and die every time I tell that lie
I cringe just thinking about you

I'm glad that I finally reached
A destination that you clearly can't get to
My vision is clear, and I can honestly say
I knew you wasn't shit
But I'll take that L

Because I gave you the benefit of the doubt
Because I saw the potential

Even when you told me yourself
You were intimidated

Intimidation Aside

I'm glad this shit didn't work out!

Late Night Dinner

Do you know what Love feels like?
Like really what does it feel like?
Is it like walking into your home
And instantly being full
Even if they aren't there
Their presence still fills the room
Even when they're not home

But you know they'll be home soon
So, you prepare
Cook, clean
And make sure everything looks neat
But then you realize it's getting late
"Where are you love?"
The questions run through your head
you don't want to call
you don't want to seem like you're bugging
But as the clock keeps showing it's getting later than late
The mind starts to race

"This nigga wants me to fuck him up"
I mean
"I hope there's nothing wrong"
I mean
"There better be a good explanation as to why he's late"

Then the clock hits 10
He walks in and
Looks at you and says
"Hey baby
I'm sorry I was working late
But I already ate"

Be Careful What You Ask For

He asked "What you gone do if I leave"

I looked at him and smiled

And said "little boy what you think"

You think I'm gonna be a sad bitch

Slinging snot

Begging for you to come back

I think the FUCK NOT

You must have forgot who you're fuckin with

So let me remind you

I'm gonna set fire to that bridge

Just in case you think you can comeback

If you leave, I'll be proud

Realizing I didn't even need yo' sorry ass anyways

Someone who wants to play games

Like a child

I'll let the world whoop you

And hopefully it cracks the man inside

Revealing that it was actually you that needed help

It was actually you that needed to question

"What if she leaves"

First Love

I remember the first time I found
out you were getting married
I tried to hide it but deep down
I died inside

I cried and stained my pillow with
mascara blackened tears
I was hurt
"What did I do to deserve this?"

I thought we were perfect
I thought I would be the one that
you would drop down on one knee
And ask if I would be yours forever

But forever came to an end
On a hot summer day
It was the day I realized that
There was no love in this space
We became distant strangers
Even though I woke up to you everyday
I cried when I saw pictures of her in
her white dress
You dressed in your tux
Your family surrounding you
Giving congratulations
As if I wasn't just in the picture
I guess I really didn't exist

Our love was nothing more than an illusion
So why did it hurt so bad
Because you were my first
I gave you parts of me
That time could never replace
I spent days praying with you
Holding your hand
Supporting anything you wanted to do

I created an image in my head
A standard of life
But didn't realize that you
would never be able to live up to it
Because it was stuck in my mind. I gave you qualities and traits
That didn't belong to you
I saw you as someone else
Instead of the person you
Showed me you were
You were just my imagination
A character

Scratched CD's

I wish I could leave you alone
Get you out of my mind
But you're stuck
Like back in 03 when the cd's
Would scratch and
That one line would be on repeat

Ode to J.Cole (Folding Clothes)

I did laundry in our love
Picked
the dirty articles up off the floor
I
stuffed them in the machine
Wishing and washing in a constant cycle
That only you and me can get clean
I'll hang this Love out to dry
For the whole world to see
Flipping and flapping in the winds
As we dry our eyes with the bedsheets
You are perfectly creased
Folded in love
Ironed and steamed with
Grace and gratitude
Your love changed my attitude about laundry
It's no longer about
Getting rid of the dirt soiled stains
Of the pain we cause each other
But it's about tossing are bullshit aside.
Doused in communication and problem solving
We wash our issues away
Air dry them for display
Then it is folded and put away

I rather be folded in love
Then to be hung up or tossed and stuffed
in the lonely darkness of
drawers and closets of our imagination

Love in 5D

My problem with love is I've been

Looking for the visual package

Someone who looks like this long list of standards

That I made up in my head

Physical attributes that don't even matter

I've been searching for love in all the wrong places

Hoping that when I see him

I would know he was the one

But now I'm understanding it's not what I see

But what I feel

Someone who makes me feel like he understands me

We fit together like puzzle pieces

We create a picture that shows what love is supposed to be

A connection with someone who holds my mind

protects my heart, and wants to create with

me

Mind

Body

and Spirit

We allow ourselves to get lost in the oneness of each other

We accept discovering love beyond the physical

We create a love that is 5th dimensional

<u>808's and Drumbeats</u>

Recycled lovers

Are like the drummer

Beating the same beat

Repetitions

Snare rifts

Beating the drum of my heartbeat

Rhythmic and in tune

Gives me the perfect beat to dance to

Things I Hold Onto are the very things I've learned to LET GO. Trauma doesn't define me. It's a reminder that I am still alive to make my journey through the human experience.

Autumn Leave

Autumn taught me

How quickly the seasons change

The changing of trees

Can leave you wondering if it's all an illusion

Do you really love me

Or am I hanging on to dead debris

Waiting to get raked up

And left for the trash man to haul me off

with the rest of the lost

Questioning Love

How do you know it's love
When everything changed so abrupt
One day I didn't know you
I spend every moment waiting to feel your touch
I spend every moment thinking about our growth
How do you know it's love
When love just decided to show up on my doorstep
Packaged in mental stimulation
Laughter, and protection
Now I spend every moment wanting to be
everything that love has to offer
Trips around the sun
Drunken nights, filled with jokes and strokes
How do you know it's love
When love was attracted so suddenly
I spent countless nights and days learning how to love me
Just to send out the signal that
I am ready to receive reciprocated energy
I created love within me
Buried it deep down into my
subconscious so that I can be the magnet
Karma came back around
to show me where all my love went

So I know it's love
And I'm gonna be the one you love
Because I love me and you are the reflection of me

Falling
I'm starting to think that maybe when we fell in love
Is the same time I started to hate myself

Poise-IN

She remained in pain
So, she could have a constant reminder
Of what a connection felt like
Too, afraid to remove herself from toxic love
She became poison
It was the most normal thing she could feel

6AM Love POEMS

We walked hand in hand, and it reminded me of love

It reminded what an embrace really feels like

Interlocked and intertwined

Not sure where our love lines divide

Creating a connectedness that only we can understand

The embrace of our hands is electrifying

Sending shockwaves through my body

Like stars in the galaxy

We tell a story of passion in the night

Just by us holding hands I'm no longer afraid of my thoughts

You have empowered me. Inspired me to tell the truth that

Lies within

Because when our hands touch it describes a time when love

was actually felt

Virgo Love

The greatest love I've ever known was with a Virgo
He allowed me to bare my soul
He allowed me to be honest
He asked me questions
And waited for my answers
The first night we met I instantly felt it
It was like my soul already knew him
I felt a connection I've never felt before
Is this what a soulmate feels like?
I'm pretty sure it was, I floated home
Wondering who he was
And then I finally had an opportunity to explore him
We laughed together
Shared stories from our lives
We discovered new things
Took trips
It was the first time I felt bliss in a relationship
I watched him grow
But I felt like I wasn't moving
I felt stuck in my mind. Not because of him but me
I convinced myself this is to good, to be true
Someone who doesn't need
Anything from you
Just wants you to be YOU
But I didn't know who I was yet
Just a young girl still discovering life
I thought I needed to make a change
But I didn't want to disturb his growth
So, I ran away. To a faraway place
Leaving love where it stood

I thought I was doing the best for me
The best for him
But all these years later
I'm still thankful for the chance
To know that kind of love
He was the definition of my opposite
But we were whole

Lost Lover

How long do I have to wait patiently?
For you to recognize that you're
supposed to be in this space with me

I know I said I needed a break
To take some time to get my spirit right
To clear my mind

But now I'm left in this cold room
This empty bed
The laughter stopped
And I have no one to share my dreams with

I want love but I was too
afraid of how you might receive that
For me to put my heart on the line
I'm telling you I need you
But I'm afraid you might think
That I'm just
Playing mind games
One day I say come closer
The next I'm pushing you further away

I convinced myself we need closure
Yes, I said we
Because I know you really didn't want this to be over
But I was stuck in my head
To stubborn to express my thoughts
Not wanting to come off overly clingy
So, I left our love to rot

My soul screamed out
I need you
But my heart said make him wait
You'll know if he's the right one
If he comes back
But you didn't
I shoved you out the door
And you never turned around
To see if I really meant it

THINGS I HOLD ONTO

And that had my mind fucked up
Like damn maybe I was the only one
Who thought this was real love

But the more I thought about it
The more I recognized
where I messed up
I was covered in my insecurities
And I tried to push them off on you
As if you were going to be able
to save me from drowning

I made love unbearable because I was lost and confused
Thinking you were too good for me
Questioning why you even wanted me

I thought you were the right person
It was just the wrong time
But now I know
You were the right person
I just had the wrong mind
Lost lover
Come back to me

Venom

Who are you, I asked him,
His response
"I am venom"
Or at least that's what I thought I heard

Museums

I circled back trying to figure out
exactly where I started from
Right back in this space again
It's familiar
Like the emptying of my stomach from a long night of drinking
I tell myself I'll never do it again
I make false promises
But I keep finding myself right back here
It's me
It has to be
I'm the common denominator
In this equation
Trying not to get my heart broken
Instead it's stolen
Ripped out of my chest
And put on display
And the caption reads
"Here is the heart of a lover. She couldn't seem to keep it for herself so she loaned it to others"

CHAPTER 3
HOLDING ONTO…

SACRED ENERGY XCHANGE

Venus Fly Trap

Come closer

I know I hypnotize you

With the sound of my voice

And the scent of my skin

I smell like

Cinnamon and honey

On a fresh Sunday morning

Can I entice you

To taste me

Don't be timid

Don't be shy

I love a man that is strong

Strong in the mind

Someone that can open me wide

Have me releasing my juices

Letting you drink freely

Lucid dreaming on a summer breeze

They call me the most

Wonderful plant in the world

The goddess of beauty

The Venus fly trap

I devour anything that gets too close to me

Loving me from A-Z

Arching my
Body it's
Calling for you to
Discover every inch with
Electric energy through your
Fingertips touching my flesh
Gasping
Hands grasping my throat
Intoxicatingly creating
Juices that flow
Kisses sweet and deep
Long
Mouthwatering strokes
Nestled between the
Opening of my
Pink flower
Quiet moans
Release as I
Stare into your eyes while you savor the
Taste between my thighs
Unleashing
Velvety vibrations of
Wet pools
Yummy Yoni juices
Xchanging our energy
Zapping me into ecstasy

Fingerprints

Our hands tell a story
Of secrets hidden behind words not spoken
Our connection
With interlocked fingers
Sharing our deepest meanings
I examine your hand
The lines show me the path to your heart
Our love is peace found between the stars
I want to hold your hand forever
Feeling the warmth of your touch
Your fingerprints left imprinted on my skin

THINGS I HOLD ONTO

<u>Secret Lover</u>

I miss you

Your soft touch

The way you would let me lay my head on your chest

After a bad day

The sound of your heartbeat

It's better than a symphony

It beats faster when I kiss your lips

Taking your face into my hands

The feeling is so passionate

I miss you

The words escape my lips

Before I have chance to even think

Guiding my legs around your waist

The way you would stroke my body

Taking your time

Finding a rhythm

That rocks us both into sexual ecstasy

I suppress screaming out your name

While we play in between the sheets

I fantasize about you

Fucking me wild

Feeding my mind

Just so I can orgasm

Cause, He doesn't do it like you

THINGS I HOLD ONTO

But I love him

Because he provides a sense of security

He wants to see the best for me

I know he'll never hurt me

Like I hurt him

But my body yearns for you

It screams for your touch

Every time he's inside of me

It recognizes

That he's not you

I guess for now we can be nothing more

Than secret lovers trapped in a secret fantasy

Harvest Season

The scent of my skin

Drips off your lips

When you plant them

Down my spine

Planting roots

Blooming fruits

Ripe enough for you

To consume

90's Kind of Love

You remind me of a late night
90's vibe
Listening to music
Getting to know each other
We're both giving each other the eye
But we remain seated
Trying not to touch each other
Do you mind if I stroke up?
The song comes on
And I'm not sure if you have mind control
Or if the universe is fucking with me
But all I can think
Is your body is calling me
I want your mouth in places
That I keep secret
Teasing me
Pleasing me
Silhouettes of our perfect frame
dancing on the ceiling
As we make love
I watch our shadows on the wall
Our energy is unmatched
It like discovering love through an
Outer body experience
I'm watching us
While watching the shadows dance
Has me feeling like we're having an orgy
You on me
Me on you
Hands and faces in places
That we hide in the dark

Silent

There is power in the way you stare at me

It reminds me love can be spoken even in S I L E N C E

<u>Drugs of Choice</u>

I'm feeling overstimulated

Slightly intoxicated

I get that way when I get too high off life

Drugs are my favorite

But it's even better when the drug is love

You give the greatest side effects

I want to be this high forever

Chasing the skies with you

Overstimulated and intoxicated off you

Treasure Box

Kisses under the covers
Like finding a box full of treasures
Hands finding secret hideaways
That leaves us both staring into each other's eyes
I hold my breath trying to suppress the moans
Neither one of us wants to look away

It's crazy that just with a simple touch
You can send a rush of blood to body
Parts that have longed for contact
I don't want to rush this moment
There's no need for penetration

I want to know how you work magic with your hands
Are you good with your hands?
You feel so good with your hands

Nice and warm
Strong enough to hold me down
But light enough to tickle the right spot
That leaves the bed soaked
And once you're finished
You put your hands in my mouth
I want to taste

Dark Knight

Your skin is as dark as the night
Your eyes are bright like the stars
You are a walking universe
Developed with love
Your touch reminds me of the sun
Warm and welcoming
Your smile reminds me of the moon
Calming and peaceful
But just enough to wake up the tides of the ocean
Moving love through gravity and space

No Hands

I love when you come home
From a long day of work
Worked up and a little tense
But nothing this mouth can't fix
As you step through the door
I know exactly what you need
It's time to release some of that stress
Put it all on me

When you walk into the bedroom
I'll be waiting
Half-naked
Just how you like me
As you pull off your shirt
I'll help you unbuckle your pants
But after that
Please move your hands

I'll start by kissing your lips
Working my way down your
neck
Your chest
Your stomach
And right before I put you in my mouth
I kiss the head to remind you
This is my dick

I'll let you penetrate my throat
Opening up my throat chakra
So, I can always express how I feel
Deep and long strokes
I may gag a bit
But I won't choke

Sloppy
And wet
I know that's how you like it
As I stare up at you
Your eyes roll back with bliss
I stop for a moment
Just so I can take some time to lick your balls
That's my favorite
I love to watch you moan and groan
Taking a handful of my hair
I suck you dry with no hands
Release the day away baby
I can handle it
I swallow
I don't spit

Night Cap

Sometimes I just want
To be sticky
And sweaty
To make love early
In the morning
Just so we can rock each
Other back to sleep again

Ode to Kendrick Lamar (Untitled-Track5)

If these walls could talk
They would sing out your name
Like background singers
As you stroke my body
Using your fingers
To trace
All the places you want to kiss first

If these walls could talk
They would tell a story
Of late nights
Early mornings
Me screaming into the pillow

If these walls could talk
They could give a playback
Blow by blow
They have seen it all
Heard it all
As we create moisture
That drips off the walls

If these walls could talk
They would say that
Our chemistry is wonderful
The way we make love is beautiful

CHAPTER 4

HOLDING ONTO …

Untitled Self-Notes

As a writer

I will spend my lifetime

Writing I LOVE YOU

In a million different ways

I pray it reaches you

THINGS I HOLD ONTO

As I cleanse my face

I wash all the bad thoughts away

I tell myself this is a new day

To make it

Everything from the past

Was a lesson

THINGS I HOLD ONTO

She is not the rose that grew from concrete
She is the sunflower that grew amongst the weeds
Her beauty is hidden
By the company she keeps
Her lips are soft
And she smells of elegance and luxury
With hues of colors
That reminds you
How great it is to be in love
The overgrowth of the weeds
That surround her
Are like old friends holding you back
From achieving all that you can be
As they are plucked away
Her thorns protect her
From the ones that want
To put her in a glass
Half full of water
Stunting her growth
Putting their love for her
On a false pedestal of display
She waits for the day
When love will greet her
Forgetting about her thorns
Because Lovers know that
Life is not exempt from pain
And pain is pleasure
Somewhere between Erykah Badu and Tupac
She grew

The alchemist is a person who transforms or creates something through a seemingly magical process.

The Alchemist taught us
That everything we are searching for
Is already within reach
Enjoy the journey!

THINGS I HOLD ONTO

I no longer answer those "are you up text"

I no longer get butterflies when you tell me "you need me"

I am no longer lost or broken

Waiting for you to put me back together again

When you finally allow yourself to Love
Accept it
Love gracefully
Love truthfully
Love with boundaries
Love with honor and respect

I want you to do more than hear me
I want you to feel me
They say life is a feeling process
For the living to experience

I put my heart on paper
Allowing myself to expose my deepest secrets
my wild thoughts and dreams

My intentions are not to get you to like me
I'm beyond that dimension of thinking
My intentions are to get you to feel
To think outside the box, you put your own mind in
To connect with your higher self
To find balance in the 5th dimension

To have yin and yang
Greet you at the door
Allowing you to explore all the possibilities of
IM-Possible

I had to learn to stop loving people by the way that I see
Them my perception of you is not real

THINGS I HOLD ONTO

I stopped having sex

Not because I don't like it

There are plenty of days and nights

I want to get tangled in bedsheets

Dripping from sweat

Heart thumping

But I had to stop

I felt like I was letting demons take over my body

Allowing them to desecrate my sacred temple

Men that really didn't know how to touch me right

They just kind of knew how to touch the right places

But even their touch felt cold

And misused

Their touch felt empty

And I wanted to feel full and whole

It was like after having sex I still desired more

My body craves more

And that's the opposite of how it should be

So, I stopped having sex

Because what I need is intimacy

I need passion

I need a touch that ignites the fire inside

Intimacy that reminds me I am alive

THINGS I HOLD ONTO

Today I surrender

I decided that today would be the day

That I provide space

For my life to grow and to reach heights

That I convinced myself was impossible

To honor myself with grace and gratitude

To sharpen my mind with words like

Swords for the battlefield

I increase my intake of love

Just by being present in the moment

Inhaling peace

Exhaling negativity

I decided to just move freely

To allow my body to contort

Letting this vessel take me to wherever it wants to be

To be free in space and time

To defy gravity

Like synergy

Connecting my higher self

With this grounded being

My body and mind flow together

Like yoga and poetry

He is more than just my man crush on Monday
He is my Sunday when I need to rest
He is my Saturday when I want to go out
He is my Friday night rooftop watching the stars align
He is my Thursday sipping wine
He is my Wednesday and I want to ride his wave
He is my Tuesday, just as beautiful as the day I was born
He is my Monday
Reminding me that no matter what day of the week
He is mine and I am his

I smile knowing that life is taking me places
My dreams imagined

THINGS I HOLD ONTO

I've been standing at the edge of the ocean
Watching as the waves crash onto the shore
I watch as they calmly
Flow back into their familiar space

I've been standing here
Waiting for you
Hoping that just like the ocean
You would flow freely to me
Hoping that you would sweep me off my feet
Bringing gifts from the bottom of the sea

I stand here hoping
That in the moment of the rush
We both get swept up with the current
Holding hands
We Flow
We float to new lands
Somewhere we can be unfamiliar faces
But a reminder of love

Pay attention!
Its invaluable money spent.
Paying attention can protect you from the dangers that lurk
From those that don't have the intentions to treat you like
They want to be treated

Read that again if you need too!

I hope that we remember who we are
In a world that wants you to hate yourself
For being yourself
oxymoron

I'm no longer afraid to be myself
Because I'm like a treasure chest
Full of diamonds and gold
Knowledge and gadgets
I had to learn that I am a multi-dimensional being

Everyone I meet has a perception of me
And quite honestly whatever you think is true
That was the self that I decided to present to you
She came out of hiding even if it was just for a moment

You get what you get
I've spent years trying to be the perfect version of me
Trying to decipher who I really am
Thinking I'm on some quest of self-discovery
But now I just laugh
At the young mind who didn't realize she is
everything

My realities are dreams fixated on thoughts never seen

I can't share them with you

I don't want to

I just want to put them on display

My words

Are My magic

It's how I create

THINGS I HOLD ONTO

The objects in the mirror may appear

Closer than what they seem

Kind of reminds me of my dreams

I know they say you just gotta believe

But what is believing when

You can't see

Or maybe it's my perception

I don't get reception here

I try to move about

Maybe finding a space

That gets full connection

But I'm just left with that damn circle

That just keeps spinning

Pretending

It wants me to find that one little bar

So I can make that call

Generational curses

I'll be the one to break them all

I am the love I needed
All those nights I found myself
broken down on the floor
Crying
Silently so no one could
Hear from outside my door

I am the love I needed
To encourage myself
To speak over myself with words
When the darkness took over
And I couldn't see what was in front of me

I am the love I needed
When you told me
Or rather showed me
That you no longer needed me
You no longer loved me

The hurt from within
Was enough to know that
I don't want to feel that kind of pain again
I wouldn't wish that on my worst enemy
Because that's the type of pain
That makes you your own worst enemy

I am the love I needed because I realized
That everything in this life is temporary
Even you
So why waste any more time crying
over something that has an expiration date

I am love
I am loved
And You are ME

Sometimes love requires
Forgetting all the pain someone put you through
Just so you can openly and freely love with pain in your heart
But faith that maybe this time things will be different

There is beauty in the way you bare your soul

Forgetting everything you were told

Don't choose your words wisely

Say them with deliberate force

Let your tongue do the whipping

Lashing at the hearts of those who find your words

Read them

Hear them

Speak your truth

I love poets because they use their words in ways most
People wouldn't
They lose the fear of how someone will feel if they said what
They said in a basic conversation
But because they use their words as art
It's acceptable
But the truth is they're just telling the truth
No matter how anyone else may sugar coat it

THINGS I HOLD ONTO

We recycle our love

Just like heaven does

As it drops tears from the sky

Watering us like plants

And then the sun comes back out

Evaporates the water waste

And what we are left with

Are human sun-kissed plants

I'm learning that there's actually no Beginning or Ending to life. Just living! Living exactly where you are in the moment.

Allowing yourself to grow and be uncomfortable.

And when things get out of control you learn to replant yourself in New Soil.

Home?

Is it a fictional place you go to

When the day is done

Home, has so many meanings

A dwelling for souls to retreat

A shelter adorned with your favorite belongings

Home. A country or state you can call your birthplace

A residence filled with love and affection

Is home truly where the heart is?

What if my physical home isn't near my spiritual home

There's that duality thing again

I'm a wanderer walking through

Only halfway feeling like I belong

I'm looking for home

Searching for a place to call my own

Not just something that I own

But a place where my life feels like it

Belongs

HAVEN'T BEEN TO SLEEP YET

MY MIND JUST WANDERS

NO REAL DESTINATION

I JUST HAVEN'T FOUND

A THOUGHT TO REST ON

What a difference life becomes
When you decide to remove
The walls that you created
And just B E L I E V E

My lesson for the day is to stop trying to figure a way out and FIND A WAY IN!

Get your shit in order so when opportunities meet you.

You are prepared.

Stay focused on your dreams

Remember the closer you get

The more you'll have people and situations

Trying to distract you by saying it's impossible

But remember their perspective isn't your reality.

I'll just sit this here for anyone who has been doubting their truth. Honestly, we are our biggest HATERS. We give all the excuses of why we "can't" do something instead of just trusting the fact that we are magic, and we literally create anything we want!

All your desires are out there. All your dreams have already come true. You just have to get out of your own way!!

Believe in You

Don't be a fool

Trying to prove to other fools

What they have already convinced themselves of knowing

THINGS I HOLD ONTO

I am a force

I am an entity

I consume

Because I am a light being

That is in love with the dark

I discovered my shadow

At one point I was too afraid to acknowledge her

But she's a part of me

There's really no way to hide from what you see

We play hide and seek

Amongst the trees

For so long I've been hearing you have to FLY in order to get to where you want to go in life. just jump off the cliff and spread your wings. but what I have been learning is the importance of standing still and GROWING

I can't be your need today
I have to focus on me

This is not your destruction

This is your rebirth.

I create poems from the stones of rock bottom

THINGS I HOLD ONTO

Fold me

Mold me

I am everything you can think of

The cream of the crop

Not just the way I look

But what I can do to you mentally

I'm your best friend, wife and sister wrapped in one

The one you can talk to about anything

The one you love unconditionally

The one you protect

Don't misuse me

Treat me well

And you will be blessed

She got through every obstacle put in her way.
With a smile and some tears. She still overcame.
She is ME

I shine bright through my flaws
They say the sparkle of a diamond depends on its flaws

While I wait for tea
I wrap my arms around my body
As tight as I can
Embracing myself with self-love
While I wait for tea
I take deep breaths
Inhaling peace and love
Exhaling negativity
Inhaling grace and gratitude
Exhaling anything that causes an attitude
While I wait for tea
I flex my toes
I wiggle my fingers
I do a couple of neck rolls
While I wait for tea
I give thanks
While I wait for tea
I close my eyes
Taking in the stillness of the moment
Reminding myself I'm still alive
I made it another day

Home has always been a place I've been searching for
A place to call my own
A place with all of my prized possessions
To have peace and solace in a home that is designed and created just for me

I question if life births us twice
Like if all the things I go through at night
Are just to build a stronger person for the daytime
To be able to put a smile on my face
To forgive and let go
To evolve into a higher being

I was birthed again using the knowledge of
My misfortune and self-torture
To inspire the world
Every night into every day is a new opportunity
To be a better version of me

I was birthed in the darkness
The darkest parts of hearts broken
Shattered like glass
Cutting deep into the flesh
To release the bright hue
of crimson flow
But I self-heal

My scars now
are story lines
that inspires others to grow

Message

Read this again when you
Begin to feel down
Remember that life is meant to teach you
But in order for you to learn
You have to make mistakes

I am a Pisces Sun and Moon and an Aquarius Rising. My purpose in life
As a poet, writer, creator; is to share my story.
The Best way I know how.

I hope that you enjoyed this Collection of Poetry as I take you on a journey of letting go trauma, unrequited love, toxic energy and discover the LOVE of SELF.

A life goal of mine is to turn my poetry into Feature Films and Network regular TV Series.

Made in the USA
Columbia, SC
04 April 2025

0103313c-147c-45d1-be24-bbeadcb070b9R01